CANON
EOS R5
POCKET GUIDE

TABLE OF CONTENTS

04 OTHER HELPFUL SETTINGS

05 STEP-BY-STEP SHOOTING INSTRUCTIONS

06 TYPICAL SHOOTING SCENARIOS

01 PRE-SHOOT CHECKLIST

Check these settings before you head out with your camera!

SETTING	MY PREFERRED SETTING
☑ Shooting Mode	....
☑ White Balance Setting	....
☑ ISO Setting	....
☑ Exposure Compensation	....
☑ Focus Mode	....
☑ Focus Method	....
☑ Drive Mode	....
☑ Metering Mode	....
☑ Picture Style	....
☑ Bracketing Setting	....
☑ Highlight Alert Setting	....
☑ File Format: RAW, JPEG, or RAW & JPEG	....
☑ Battery Fully Charged and In Camera	....
☑ Memory Card(s) Formatted and In Camera	....

02 BUTTONS, DIALS, AND SCREENS

CAMERA BODY TOP

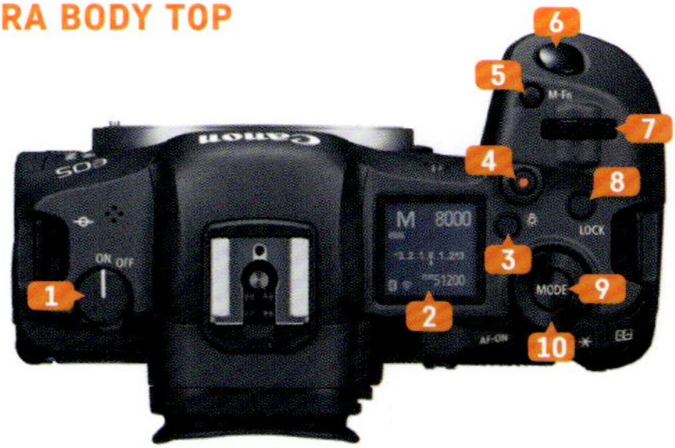

1. **Power Switch:** Turns the camera on and off.
2. **LCD Panel:** Shows basic camera information.
3. **LCD Panel Information Switch / Illumination Button:** Use to switch between views on the LCD panel / Use to illuminate the LCD panel.
4. **Movie Shooting Button:** Press to start/stop recording a movie.
5. **Multi-Function (M-Fn) Button:** Press this button in combination with turning the Quick Control Dial 1 in order to set the ISO, Drive mode, AF (autofocus) operation, White Balance, and Flash Exposure Compensation.
6. **Shutter Button:** Press halfway to activate autofocus, press all the way to take a photo.
7. **Main Dial:** Use this dial to set the shutter speed, aperture, and other settings.
8. **LOCK (Multi-Function Lock) Button:** Prevents settings from being changed if you accidentally operate the Main dial, Quick Control dial, or the lens's Control Ring.

9. Mode Button: Use with the Main Dial to select the shooting mode. To switch between still photos and movie mode, press the Mode Button, then the Info Button.

10. Quick Control Dial 2: Use this dial to set exposure compensation, aperture setting while in Manual Shooting mode, etc.

CAMERA BODY BACK

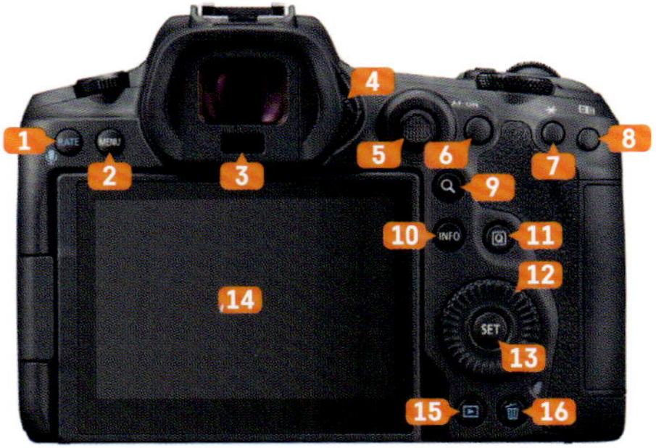

1. RATE Button / Voice Memo Button: Use to apply star rating to images during playback / Use to leave voice memos.

2. MENU Button: Press to bring up Menu options.

3. Viewfinder Sensor: Senses when you're looking through the viewfinder and activates the viewfinder display.

4. Dioptric Adjustment Knob: Turn left or right to make the viewfinder display sharp.

5. Multi-Controller: Use for operations such as white balance correction, autofocus (AF) point movement, magnifying the frame during playback, Quick Control setting adjustments, etc. Can also select or set menu items.

6. **AF Start (AF-ON) Button:** Press to engage the autofocus.
7. **AE Lock Button:** Use to lock exposure.
8. **AF Point Selection Button:** Use to select the desired autofocus (AF) point.
9. **Magnify/Reduce Button:** Use to adjust image playback options (index view, zoom in, and zoom out).
10. **INFO Button:** Press to cycle through views displaying different information.
11. **Quick Control (Q) Button:** Use to access the Quick Control screen.
12. **Quick Control Dial 1:** Use to navigate menus, move focus points, etc.
13. **SET Button:** Use to finalize a setting and return to a previous screen.
14. **Screen:** Displays multiple features, options, and settings for shooting and playback.
15. **Playback Button:** Press to view the last image taken.
16. **Erase/Trash Button:** Use to erase the current photo on display.

CAMERA BODY FRONT

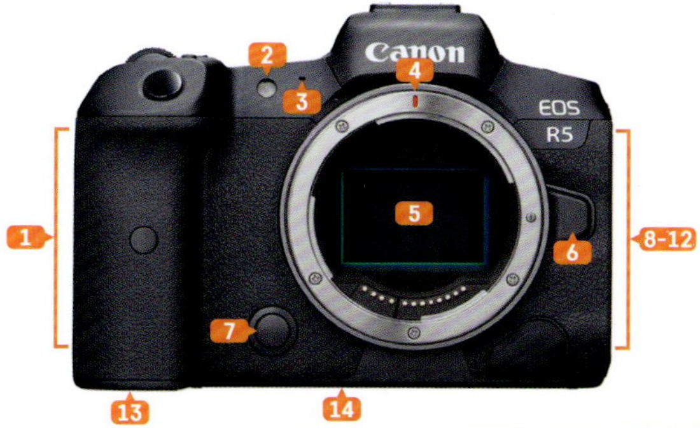

1. **Memory Card Slots and Cover:** Supports CFExpress Type B and SD/SDHC/SDXC memory cards.
2. **AF-Assist Beam/Self-Timer Lamp:** Lights up area in front of camera in low light/Blinks when Self-Timer is active.
3. **Microphones:** Records audio when recording movies.
4. **Lens Mounting Mark:** Use to line up lens and camera when mounting a lens.
5. **Image Sensor:** The 45-megapixel full-frame CMOS sensor.
6. **Lens Release Button:** Press to remove lens.
7. **Depth-of-Field Preview Button:** Press to stop down the lens to the current aperture value to show you the depth of field in the image.
8. **Microphone Terminal:** Connect an external microphone to the camera.
9. **Digital Terminal:** Connect to digital devices.
10. **HDMI Out Terminal:** Connect HDMI micro cable.
11. **Headphones:** Connect headphones to camera.
12. **PC Terminal:** Connect to remote flash units.
13. **Battery and Battery Compartment Cover:** Open to access battery compartment.
14. **Tripod Socket:** Standard socket for tripod or monopod.

SHOOTING SCREEN (STILL PHOTO)

Each time you press the INFO button, the information display will change. The display will show only the settings currently applied.

Note: Viewfinder display positions will vary for some items.

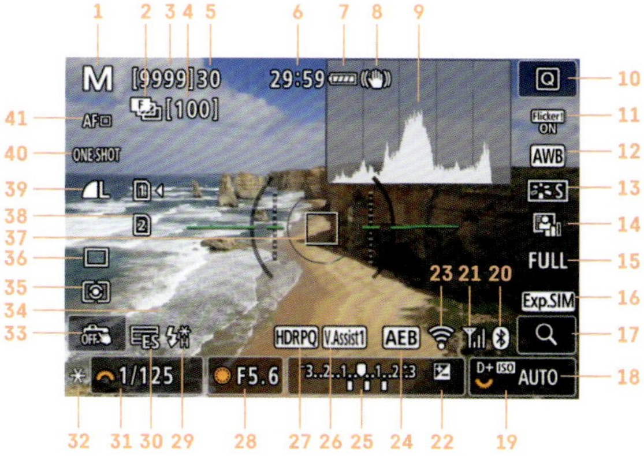

1. **Shooting Mode**
2. **Focus Bracketing/HDR/Multiple Exposures/Multi Shot Noise Reduction/Bulb Timer/Interval Timer**
3. **Possible Shots/Seconds Until Self-Timer Shoots**
4. **Number of Remaining Shots for Focus Bracketing, Multiple Exposure, or Interval Timer**
5. **Maximum Burst**
6. **Movie Recording Time Available**
7. **Battery Level**

8. Image Stabilizer
9. Histogram
10. Quick Control Button
11. Anti-Flicker Shooting
12. White Balance/White Balance Correction
13. Picture Style
14. Auto Lighting Optimizer
15. Still Photo Cropping/Aspect Ratio
16. Exposure Simulation
17. Magnify Button
18. ISO Speed
19. Highlight Tone Priority
20. Bluetooth Function
21. Wi-Fi Signal Strength
22. Exposure Compensation
23. Wi-Fi Function
24. AEB/FEB (Auto Exposure Bracketing/Flash Exposure Bracketing)
25. Exposure Level Indicator
26. View Assist
27. HDR PQ
28. Aperture Value
29. Flash Ready/FE (Flash Exposure) Lock/High-Speed Sync
30. Electronic Shutter
31. Shutter Speed
32. AE (Auto Exposure) Lock
33. Touch Shutter/Create Folder
34. Multi-Function Lock Warning
35. Metering Mode
36. Drive Mode
37. AF Point (1-Point AF)
38. Memory Card
39. Image Quality
40. AF Operation
41. AF Method

SHOOTING SCREEN (MOVIE)

Each time you press the INFO button, the information display will change. The display will show only the settings currently applied.

Note: Viewfinder display positions will vary for some items.

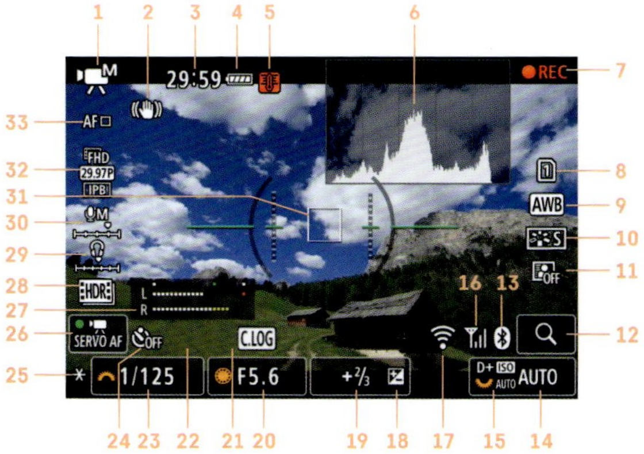

1. Movie Shooting Mode
2. Image Stabilizer
3. Movie Recording Time Available/Elapsed Recording Time
4. Battery Level
5. Temperature Warning
6. Histogram (Brightness/RGB)
7. Recording In Progress

8. Memory Card Used for Recording/Playback
9. White Balance/White Balance Correction
10. Picture Style
11. Auto Lighting Optimizer
12. Magnify Button
13. Bluetooth Function
14. ISO Speed
15. Highlight Tone Priority
16. Wi-Fi Signal Strength
17. Wi-Fi Function
18. Exposure Compensation
19. Exposure Level Indicator (Metering Levels)
20. Aperture Value
21. Canon Log
22. Multi-Function Lock Warning
23. Shutter Speed
24. Movie Self-Timer
25. AE (Auto Exposure) Lock
26. Movie Servo AF
27. Audio Recording Level Indicator (Manual/Line Input)
28. HDR Movie
29. Headphone Volume
30. Audio Recording Level (Manual/Line Input)
31. AF Point (1-point AF)
32. Movie Recording Size
33. AF Method

03 ESSENTIAL MODES AND SETTINGS

SHOOTING MODES

Press the Mode button and rotate the Quick Control Dial 2 to select the desired Shooting mode.

A+ (Scene Intelligent Auto): The camera assesses the scene and sets the optimum settings automatically. It will even adjust the focus on both still and moving subjects.

Fv (Flexible-Priority AE): Shutter speed, aperture, and ISO are all set automatically, then you can change one, two, or all three settings to get the desired exposure. The settings you don't change will automatically be adjusted by the camera.

P (Program AE): The camera sets the shutter speed and aperture based on metering info and current ISO.

Tv (Time Value, or Shutter Speed Priority): You set the shutter speed and the camera sets the aperture based on metering info and current ISO.

Av (Aperture Value, or Aperture Priority): You set the aperture, and the camera sets the shutter speed based on metering info and current ISO. Range of available apertures depends on the attached lens.

M (Manual): You set ISO, shutter speed, and aperture. Refer to the exposure level indicator.

Bulb: Used for long exposures, the shutter stays open as long as you hold down the shutter button. Use the Main dial to set the aperture.

C1, C2, C3 (Custom Shooting Modes): Use the Set-Up Menu to set a custom shooting mode.

Movie: Use to record movies.

METERING MODES

Press the Q button, then use one of the Quick Control dials to navigate to and select a Metering mode.

Evaluative: General-purpose mode suited for most situations and subjects (even backlit subjects).

Partial: Uses 5.8% of the area at the center of the screen for determining exposure. Good choice when there is very bright light around the subject.

Spot: Uses 2.9% of the area at the center of the screen. Use when you need to meter on a specific part of the scene.

Center-Weighted Average: The camera analyzes the whole scene to determine exposure, but places more emphasis on info at the center of the screen.

EXPOSURE COMPENSATION

Press Shutter button halfway down, then rotate the Quick Control Dial 1 to adjust exposure compensation, from −3 (darker) to +3 (lighter) stops, in 1/3-stop increments. When shooting in the Fv Shooting mode, you set the exposure compensation by rotating the Quick Control Dial 2 to select Exposure Level indicator, then using the Main dial to set the exposure compensation. To reset the exposure compensation back to 0, press the Erase/Trash button.

Note: The exposure compensation you set will remain in effect until you change it; it does not return to 0 when the camera is turned off.

FOCUS OPERATION

MENU > AF (Screen 1) > AF Operation

One Shot AF: Focus starts when Shutter button is pressed halfway, then locks when focus is achieved. Best for stationary subjects.

Servo: Focus starts when Shutter button is pressed halfway and continues to focus until photo is taken. Best for moving subjects.

Note: For **Manual focus**, set the AF/MF switch on the lens to MF, and rotate the focus ring on the lens barrel to focus.

AUTOFOCUS METHODS

MENU > AF (Screen 1) > AF Method

Face+Tracking: The camera automatically detects and focuses on human or animal faces.

Spot AF: The camera focuses on the smallest possible area, even narrower than 1-Point AF.

1-Point AF: The camera focuses using a single point for critical focus.

Expand AF Area: The camera uses one AF point, as well as the points adjacent and nearby to that focus point to help focus. Helpful for moving subjects that are difficult to track with 1-Point AF.

Expand AF Area: Around: The camera creates an even larger area around one AF point to find focus.

Zone AF: The camera automatically picks focus point using a large area. Generally will focus on the nearest subject.

Large Zone AF: Vertical: Like Zone AF, but camera selects the focus point from a vertical zone.

Large Zone AF: Horizontal: Like Zone AF, but camera selects the focus point from a horizontal zone.

ADDITIONAL AUTOFOCUS OPTIONS

Move the AF point or Zone AF frame: Press the AF Point Selection button, then use the Multi-Controller to move the point to the desired location and press the Set button. To center the AF point, press the Multi-Controller straight in. You can also tap directly on the screen to select the focus point.

Eye Detection: MENU > AF (Screen 1) > Eye Detection. Select Enable to have the camera automatically attempt to find focus directly on the subject's eyes when the AF method is set to Face+Tracking.

Subject to Detect: MENU > AF (Screen 1) > Subject to Detect. You can specify what type of subject is tracked when the AF method is Face+Tracking, Zone AF, or Large Zone AF (both Vertical and Horizontal). The choices are People, Animals, or No Priority.

Manual Focus Peaking: MENU > AF (Screen 2) > MF Peaking Settings. When manually focusing, focus peaking informs you that focus has been achieved by lighting up when edges of subject are in focus.

DRIVE MODES

Press the M-Fn (Multi-Function) button and rotate the Quick Control Dial 1 to select Drive Mode option, then rotate Main dial to select the desired mode.

Single Shooting: The camera takes a single shot every time Shutter button is fully pressed.

High-Speed Continuous Shooting +: The camera takes up to 12 frames per second when you press and hold the Shutter button.

High-Speed Continuous Shooting: The camera takes up to 8 frames per second (6 frames per second when using Mechanical Shutter mode) when you press and hold the Shutter button.

Low-Speed Continuous Shooting: The camera takes up to 3 frames per second when you press and hold the Shutter button.

Self-Timer 10: Sets the self-timer for 10 seconds.

Self-Timer 2: Sets the self-timer for 2 seconds.

SHUTTER MODE

MENU > Shooting (screen 6) > Shutter Mode.

Mechanical: Uses the mechanical shutter, recommended when shooting wide open with fast glass.

Electronic 1st-curtain: The front curtain opens silently; taking the photos uses the mechanical rear curtain.

Electronic: This uses the electronic curtain for the whole photograph with no shutter noise and a higher frames per second (20/fps), but shutter speeds slower than 0.5 sec are not available. Images of fast-moving subjects may distort. Flash photography is not available.

WHITE BALANCE

Press the M-Fn (Multi-Function) button and rotate the Quick Control Dial 1 to select the White Balance option, then rotate Main dial to select the desired setting.

Auto (AWB) (Ambience Priority) setting is best for most situations. **AWB-W** (White Priority) is best when you want to reduce a warm color cast. White balance can be set to shift colors warmer, cooler, or keep them accurate. Other settings are all matched to different lighting types. For truest colors, pick the type of lighting being used to illuminate scene.

FILE FORMATS

MENU > Shooting (Screen 1) > Image Quality. Use the Main dial to select the RAW quality, and use the Quick Control Dial 1 to select the JPEG quality.

RAW/C-RAW (Compact RAW): The RAW data from the image sensor is recorded each time a photo is taken. The C-RAW version is a compressed RAW file that takes up less space.

RAW/JPEG: If you have selected both a RAW and JPEG option, the camera saves two files each time the Shutter button is pressed: a RAW file and a JPEG file. You also decide the size of the JPEG (fine, normal, large, medium, small).

JPEG: The camera saves a JPEG file each time the Shutter button is pressed. You also decide the size of the JPEG.

HEIF: This file type is used for HDR photography and can be converted to JPEG after shooting.

04 OTHER HELPFUL SETTINGS

EXPOSURE SIMULATION

MENU > Shooting (Screen 7) > Exposure Simulation. This feature displays a simulation of the current exposure settings as they are applied to the scene.

Enable: The displayed image brightness will be close to the actual exposure of the resulting image. Exposure compensation will change the simulated brightness of the image accordingly.

During: Shows the exposure simulation only when you press the button that is assigned to Depth-of-Field Preview. To do this, go to MENU > Custom Functions (Screen 3) > Customize Buttons.

Disable: Exposure Simulation is essentially off. The image is displayed at the standard brightness all the time, regardless of exposure settings or exposure compensation.

PICTURE STYLES

MENU > Shooting (Screen 3) > Picture Style

Allows you to adjust settings for JPEG images. Adjustable settings are Sharpness (Strength, Fineness, Threshold),

Contrast, Saturation, Color Tone, Filter Effect (Monochrome), and Toning Effect (Monochrome). Seven preset picture controls can all be adjusted: **A (Auto), S (Standard), P (Portrait), L (Landscape), FD (Fine Detail), N (Neutral), F (Faithful), M (Monochrome)**. The Monochrome also has four color filters: Yellow, Orange, Red, Green. Finally, there are also three User-Defined Picture Styles, which allow you to customize any of the styles for easy access.

CUSTOM WHITE BALANCE

Setting a custom White Balance can help you get the best color when you're shooting under mixed lighting:

1. Take a photo of a white card (or white wall) under the mixed lighting at the scene. Be sure to fill the screen (this may require you to switch to manual focus to create the exposure).

2. Select MENU > Shooting (Screen 3) > Custom White Balance.

3. The last photo taken will be shown (if not, select it with the Quick Control Dial 1), and press SET. Select OK.

4. Select MENU > Shooting (Screen 3) > White Balance, and select the Custom White Balance icon.

COLOR SPACE

MENU > Shooting (Screen 3) > Color Space

sRGB: Smaller color space. Best when images are used directly from camera.

Adobe RGB: Larger color space. Best used when images will be edited with post-processing software.

HIGHLIGHT ALERT (BLINKIES)

MENU > Playback (Screen 5) > Highlight Alert

Select Enable so that clipped highlights will blink, alerting you to possible overexposure when playing back images. To obtain more detail in those areas, adjust exposure settings or exposure compensation and shoot again.

NOISE REDUCTION

MENU > Shooting (Screen 4) > Long Exposure Noise Reduction

Reduces noise in images with shutter speeds of 1 second or longer. Doubles time needed to save image to memory card. Choices are Auto, Enable, and Disable. Auto is usually the best choice.

MENU > Shooting (Screen 4) > High ISO Speed NR

Reduces noise in images taken at high ISO settings. Use Standard for default, Low for less noise reduction, and High for more noise reduction. Only affects JPEG images.

AUTO ISO

MENU > Shooting (Screen 2) > ISO Speed Settings

Within the ISO Speed Settings, you can select Auto for the ISO Speed, then use the Auto Range option to set the minimum and maximum ISO settings to define the range that the camera can use. You can also set the Minimum Shutter Speed to ensure that the camera does not lower the shutter speed too much; this helps reduce camera shake and blurry images.

EXPOSURE BRACKETING

You can bracket a set of three exposures up to +/-3 stops in 1/3-stop increments:

1. Select MENU > Shooting (Screen 2) > Exposure Compensation/AEB.
2. Set the Bracketing range by turning the Main dial.
3. If desired, set the exposure compensation amount by turning the Quick Control Dial 1. Press Set.

4. Take the pictures, and three bracketed shots will be created. (If you're in Single shooting drive mode, take three pictures to create the bracketed sequence. If you're in a Continuous shooting drive mode, the three shots will be taken together when you press and hold the Shutter button.)

Note: Bracketing will remain on until you set the Bracketing range back to 0.

WIRELESS CONNECTION

Install the Camera Connect app on your smartphone and pair it with the EOS R5.

This will allow you to view and transfer images to your smartphone, see the Live View image on your smartphone, and even shoot remotely from your smartphone.

RESET CAMERA

MENU > Set-Up (Screen 5) > Reset Camera

Select Basic Settings to restore the default settings for the shooting functions and menu settings. Select Other Settings in order to choose individual settings to reset to their default settings.

MULTIPLE EXPOSURES

Create in-camera multiple exposures:

1. Select MENU > Shooting (Screen 5) > Multiple Exposure.
2. Choose a shooting option:

   On: Function/Control: Choose this if you want to shoot gradually and check the results as you shoot.

   On: Continuous Shooting: Choose this if you're shooting continuous multiple exposures of moving subjects.
3. Choose a Multiple Exposure Control option:

   Additive: The exposure of each image is added cumulatively.

   Average: Based on the number of exposures you set (next step), negative exposure compensation is added automatically as you shoot to achieve a standard overall exposure.

   Bright: Retains brightest portion of images.

   Dark: Retains darkest portion of images.
4. Set the number of exposures you'd like to combine, then press Set.
5. Specify whether you'd like to save all the individual images or just the resulting multiple exposure.

6. Set a Continue Multiple Exposure option:

   1-Shot Only: Shoot just one multiple exposure.

   Continuously: Continue shooting multiple exposures until you disable the feature.

7. Shoot all of the exposures to combine into one multiple exposure. ***Note:*** As you shoot, press the Depth-of-Field Preview button to show the current exposure and how the images look merged together. When shooting using the Function/Control method (step 2), press the Playback button after taking individual shots for additional options (such as deleting the previous image so you can recapture a shot).

HDR **HDR**

Combine three images to reduce the contrast and improve tonal range. The Canon EOS R5 generates one JPEG image as the resulting HDR image:

1. Select MENU > Shooting (Screen 5) > HDR Mode.
2. Choose the dynamic range you want:

   Auto: Sets the dynamic range automatically depending on the scene's tonal range.

   +/–1, +/–2, or +/–3: The higher the number, the wider the dynamic range of the image will be.

3. Set an Effect:

Natural: Preserves wide tonal range.

Art Standard: The picture will look a bit more like a painting.

Art Vivid: More saturated colors.

Art Bold: Most saturated colors.

Art Embossed: Saturation, brightness, contrast, and gradation are decreased for an overall flat image. Creates a faded and old look.

4. Select an option for Continuous HDR:

1 Shot Only: You'll only shoot one HDR image.

Every Shot: You'll keep shooting HDR images until you disable HDR shooting by selecting MENU > Shooting (Screen 5) > HDR Mode > Disable HDR.

5. Select the Auto Image Align setting:

Enable: Choose this if you're shooting handheld.

Disable: Choose if you're shooting on a tripod.

6. Determine if you'd like to save all the images that you shoot or just the resulting HDR image with the Save Source Images option.

7. Take the picture.

TIME-LAPSE MOVIES

Create a time-lapse movie in-camera:

1. Select MENU > Shooting (Screen 5) > Time-Lapse Movie, and choose Enable.
2. Select Interval and enter both the shooting duration and the movie duration.
3. Set the Number of Shots you'd like to take for the time-lapse movie.
4. Select the desired Movie Recording Size (8K, 4K, or Full HD).
5. Select Auto Exposure to choose the shooting method:

   Fixed 1st Frame: The first shot is metered, then all subsequent shots match that first shot's exposure.

   Each Frame: Each frame is metered and shot separately.
6. In the Screen Auto Off option, choose Disable to have the image displayed (though the screen will automatically turn off 30 minutes after the time-lapse shooting begins); choose Enable to have the screen turn off 10 seconds after the time-lapse shooting begins.

Note: You can press the INFO button at any time during time-lapse shooting to turn on and off the screen.

7. Choose whether you'd like to hear a beep after every image is captured (Beep as Image Taken).

8. Once all these settings are selected, press MENU to turn off the menu screen.

9. A message will come on screen prompting you to take a test shot. Press OK, and take a test shot or two to make sure the correct focus and exposure are set.

10. Press the Movie Shooting button, then press the Shutter button to start shooting the time-lapse movie.

06 TYPICAL SHOOTING SCENARIOS

SHOOTING SCENARIO
PORTRAIT

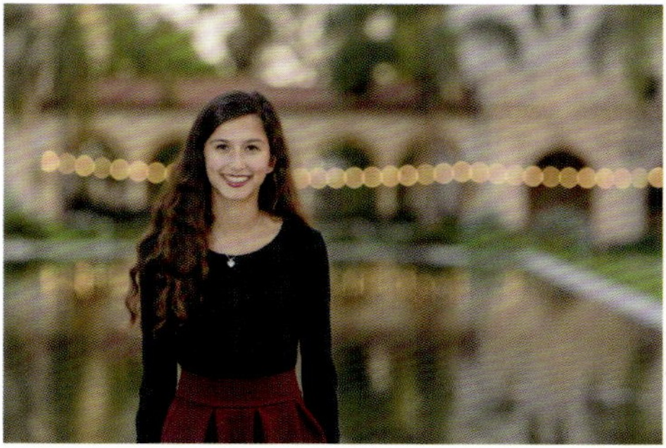

KEY PRINCIPLES

- The key to a portrait like this is shallow depth of field. So shoot in **APERTURE PRIORITY (Av)** mode and start with the lowest aperture your lens offers (such as **f/2.8 or f/4**).
- Remember to **focus on the eyes**.
- If the image is too dark or too light, use **EXPOSURE COMPENSATION** to adjust the brightness level.

- If the image is blurry from a slow shutter speed, **raise the ISO** to increase your sensor's sensitivity to light, thus allowing for a faster shutter speed.
- Remember to use a **focal length of 50mm or greater** so that you don't distort your subject's face.

SHOOTING SCENARIO
GROUP PORTRAIT

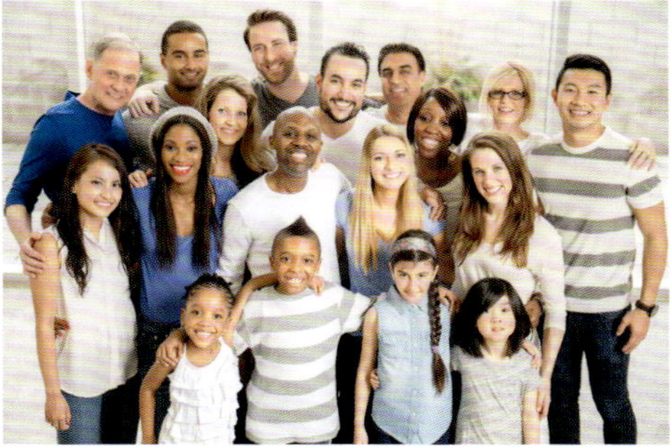

KEY PRINCIPLES

- In order to get everyone in focus, you need a deep depth of field. So shoot in **APERTURE PRIORITY (Av)** mode and set the aperture between **f/8–f/16**.

- **Focus on the person in the middle of the group**. Check the focus by using the LCD screen. View it at 100% and check faces in the front and back rows. If anyone is out of focus, use a smaller aperture for deeper depth of field.
- Use **EVALUATIVE METERING** to account for the light in the entire scene.
- **Arrange the group so they can all see you** (and you can see them).
- Use **EXPOSURE COMPENSATION** if the image is too bright or too dark.
- If image is blurry, **raise the ISO** to allow the camera to use a faster shutter speed.

SHOOTING SCENARIO

LANDSCAPE

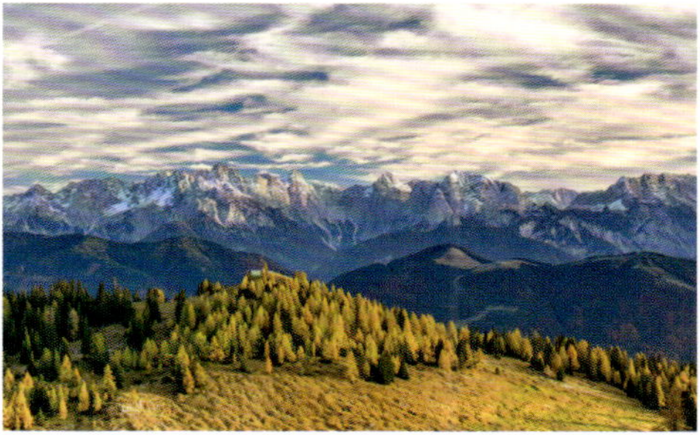

KEY PRINCIPLES

- Shoot in **APERTURE PRIORITY (Av) mode** to control depth of field, and start with **f/16** to ensure deep depth of field.
- **Use a tripod** to eliminate camera movement. Whenever your camera is on a tripod, also make sure that any **IMAGE STABILIZATION** is turned off.
- Use **EVALUATIVE METERING** and **ONE SHOT AF** focus mode.
- **Set the ISO to a low setting (100–200)** to avoid any digital noise.
- Shoot in **RAW** so that you have the most available information when editing later.
- Consider **BRACKETING** your exposures.

SHOOTING SCENARIO

FREEZE ACTION

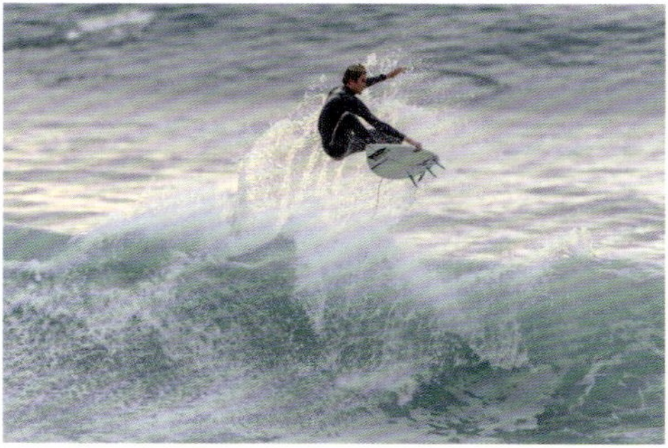

KEY PRINCIPLES

- Use **SHUTTER PRIORITY (Tv)** mode and set the shutter speed to a value that will freeze the action. The appropriate shutter speed depends on your subject and its movement, but could be anywhere between **1/500–1/8000 sec**.
- Use **SERVO** autofocus so that the camera keeps focusing as the subject moves.
- If the image is dark or blurry, **raise the ISO or try AUTO ISO** to automatically have the camera adjust the ISO as needed.

SHOOTING SCENARIO

SHOWING MOTION—PANNING

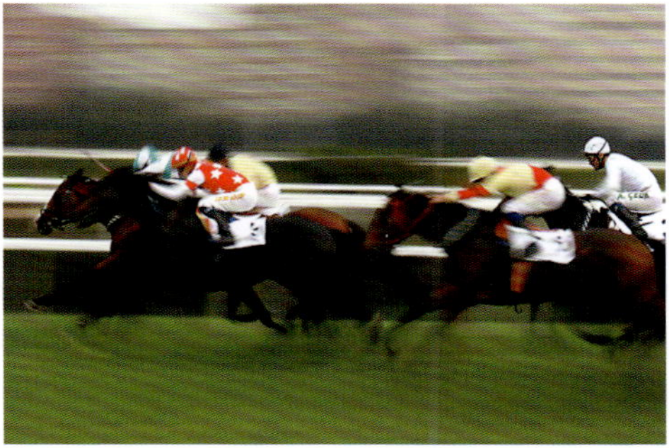

KEY PRINCIPLES

- Shoot in **SHUTTER PRIORITY (Tv)** mode and use a slow-enough shutter speed to allow for the subject to move during the exposure.
- **Follow the subject** across the frame as you shoot.
- Use **SERVO** autofocus, as well as the **EXPAND AF AREA** focus mode to ensure the camera focuses on the subject.

SHOOTING SCENARIO

LOW-LIGHT ACTION

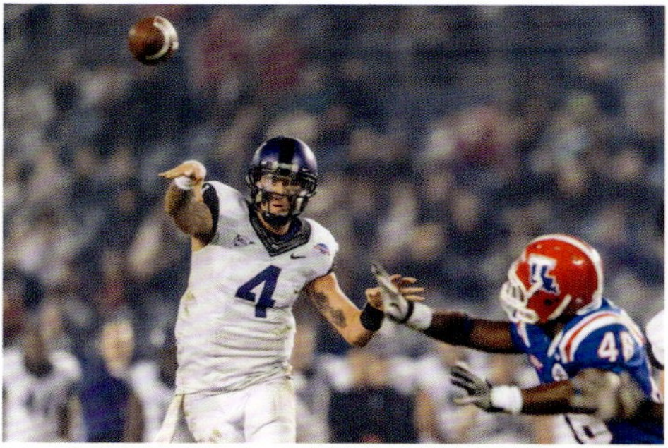

KEY PRINCIPLES

- Shoot in **APERTURE PRIORITY (Av)** mode and use a wide aperture such as **f/2.8 or f/4**.
- Use **PARTIAL METERING** and meter on the subject's face.
- Use **SERVO** autofocus and **1-POINT AF** (a single focus point).
- **Set the ISO to 1600 or higher**, depending on the amount of available light.
- If the image is blurry, **increase the ISO** to allow for a faster shutter speed.

SHOOTING SCENARIO

LONG EXPOSURE

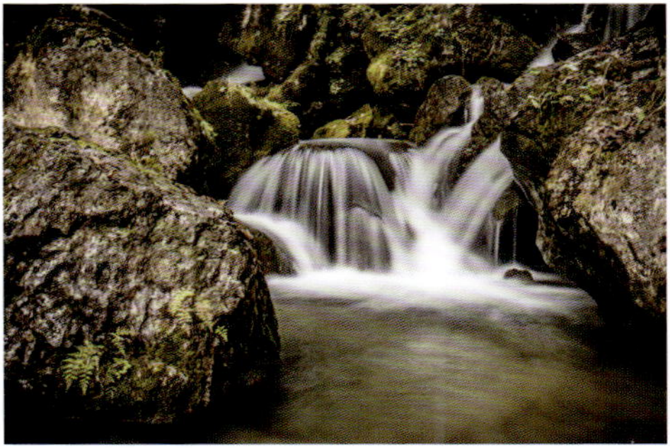

KEY PRINCIPLES

- Use **MANUAL** or **BULB** shooting mode so you can use a long shutter speed.
- **Use a tripod** to keep the camera stable. **Turn off any IMAGE STABILIZATION**.
- Use the **ONE SHOT AF** focus mode, or try manual focus if the camera is having a hard time locking on focus.
- **Use a low ISO** (100–400) and **shoot RAW** to ensure a high-quality file.
- Use a **cable release** with a lock to avoid touching (shaking) the camera.

SHOOTING SCENARIO

MACRO/CLOSE-UP

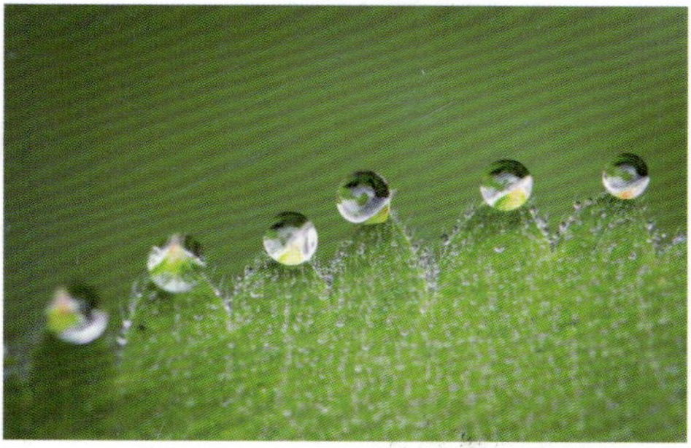

KEY PRINCIPLES

- Shoot in **APERTURE PRIORITY (Av)** mode and **use a small aperture** to ensure you achieve enough depth of field (this image was shot at f/13).
- Use **EVALUATIVE METERING** to analyze the light in the entire frame.
- A **tripod** is very useful for keeping the camera steady.
- Use **MANUAL FOCUS** and **zoom in** to confirm your focus is tack-sharp.
- Try using a dedicated **macro lens** or **close-up filters** to make sure you can achieve sharp focus when you're so close to the subject.